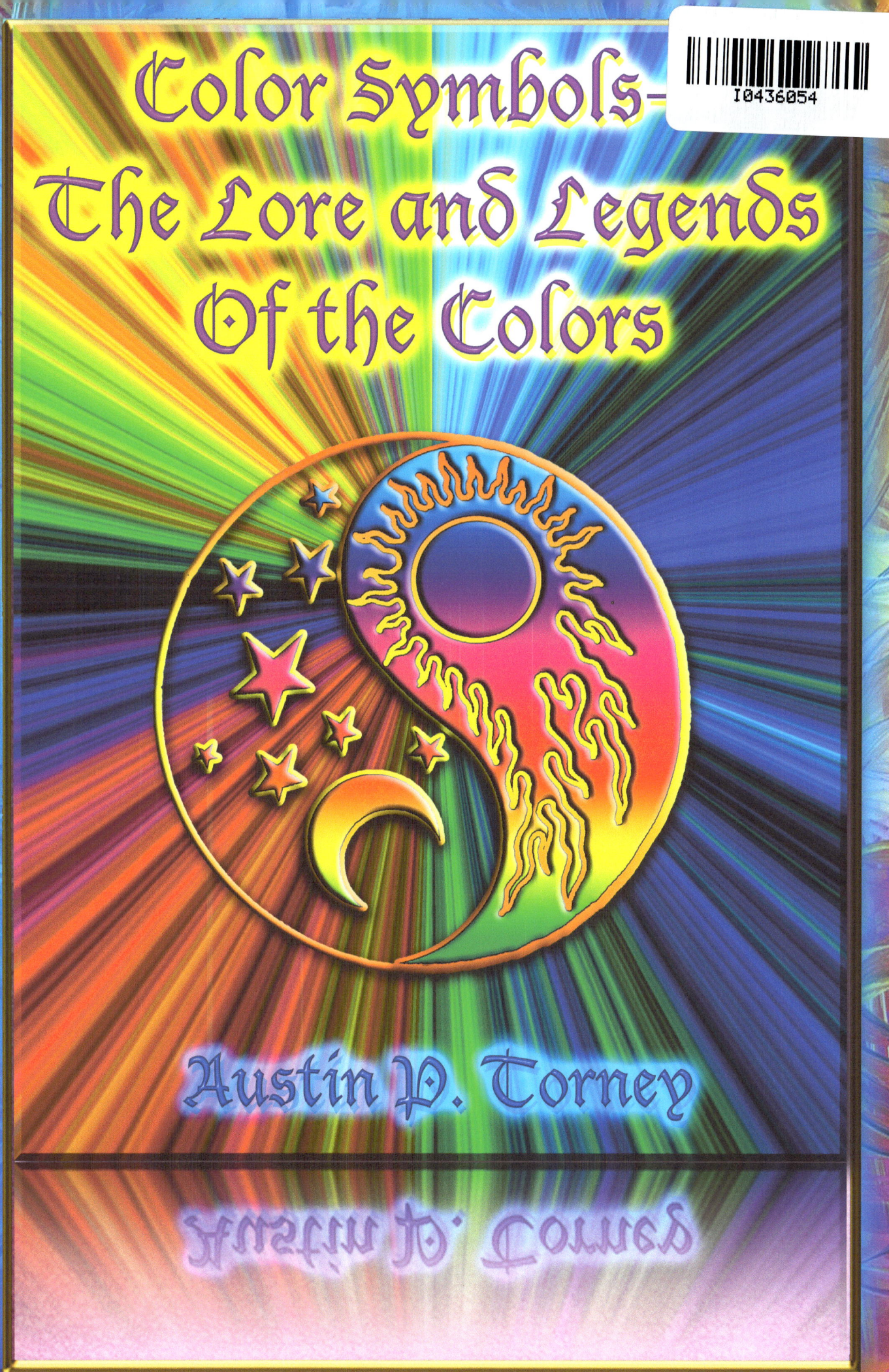

# Color Symbols— The Lore and Legends Of the Colors

## Austin P. Torney

In the nether world I learned the lore and
Legends of the colors, of their uses
In nature and emotions, the whatfor
Of their light's glowing activity:

All color variants, quite numberless,
Are made from the three primaries, no less;
Namely: red, yellow, and blue—often backed
By colorless white tinges or shades of black.

From just these three essential hues derives
All the heaven's prismatic radiance,
Myriad colors of floral brilliance,
And technicolors that seem so alive.

The offspring of married red and yellow
Is the secondary, orange, a bright fellow;
Its sibling, of blue and yellow, is green,
With of course some gradation in between.

Saintly brother purple, twixt reds and blues,
Completes the second generation hues.
Next to arrive, lime-green, is a grandchild,
As are all the tertiary colors wild—

They're crimson, magenta, maroon, scarlet,
Amber, auburn, salmon, ocher, russet,
Mauve, taupe, fuchsia, cherry, cerise, umber,
Teal, emerald, and vermilion others.

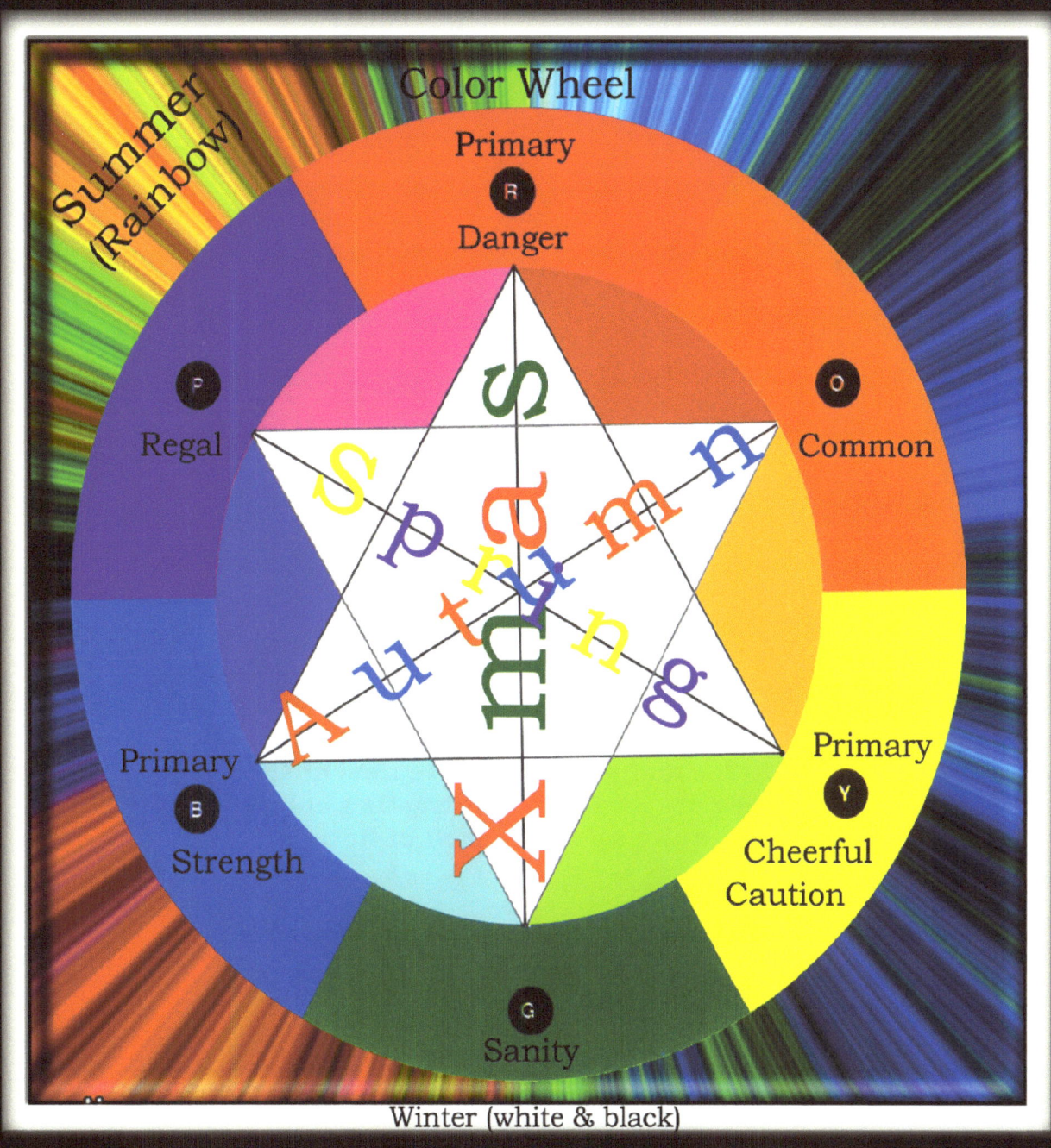

**Color Wheel**

Summer (Rainbow)

Primary
R
Danger

Regal — P

Common — O

Primary
B
Strength

Primary
Y
Cheerful
Caution

G
Sanity

Spring
Summer
Autumn
Xmas

Winter (white & black)

Strangely enough, all the color-pairs
That symbolize seasons and festive fairs,
As they're found naturally in nature's ways,
Do contrast on the color wheel, crossways:

Direct opposites on the color wheel,
Sky-blue and leafy-orange represent fall,
For they are autumn's contrasting colors—
That quite up for its lack of flowers.

As with crocus, spring's floral colors yet
Remain yellow primrose, purple violet—
The sensual sun, as it were, warming
The virginal earth, with love, into spring.

The Christmas Holiday Season's scene
Is of opposing hues of red and green—
As in Holly, berry-red, ever-green,
Or in Poinsettias' red flush, leaf of green.

*We're out of diametric color sets,*
*So which for summer? It must then contain*
The entire spectrum, as these the sunset
And the rainbow express in shine and rain.

Since winter's snow hides all things out of sight,
Its colors are hidden inside white and night—
The cold season's symbols, for they conceal
All of spring's and summer's bright floral feel.

For that as different as day and night,
We have the twin-opposites: black and white;
For the day-clock first became dark and light
When twin-gods split day and night, wrong and right.

Heaven's splendor, white, for purity, bless,
Holds all the colors of prismatic light,
But the symbol of the Prince of Darkness,
Black, removes all the colors from our sight.

So then, it is proved that in both nature
And in the color wheel opposites attract
And complement in their contrast—to procure
Both real and symbolic color contracts.

Next we'll turn to the colors lone, to see
The whatfor of their light's activity,
But first, let's ask, *Are there any missing hues,
Unknown, hidden in rainbows, or not used?*

*Hidden colors?* No, for I see how red goes
To orange, graduating through the rainbow
Into yellow and on through green, to let
Blue into indigo to become violet.

Perhaps between green and blue, lies some new
Tincture unique enough to be it's own hue,
But alas, those turquoise waves everyday
In tropic seas wash that theory away.

Yet there may be some new colors that lie
Before or beyond the spectrum and the eye,
Like infrared or ultraviolet,
Or gold, which only the fairies can see.

But what of clear, white, silver, gray, or black?
Well, they're not true colors, for, either they lack
All color (black, clear) or hide all hues (white)
Or are mixtures (gray, silver): black-white.

But wait, there is a well-known color,
One quite common in both dress and nature,
That cannot be found in the rainbow—
Give up? It's brown—and has nowhere to go!

Brown is the color of death, like the leaves
That crumble dry and lifeless when earth grieves,
Which is why the faeries won't let it show
In their magically spectral rainbow.

But alas, brown's new hue is not to last,
For brown's no more than red, yellow, and black.
So onward we move: *What do colors mean?*
*What's nature's physiological scheme?*

When we see red, we see danger: *Stop! Blood!*
Metabolism rises, adrenaline floods—
And so restaurants use red tablecloths
To increase both the appetite and the cost.

Yellow, the quickest color we can see,
Means caution, as with black on a bee,
But yellow's bright and cheerful too, and lends
Light to small and sunless rooms like kitchens.

Healthful orange is the common man's color;
So to make the expensive look cheaper,
Such as with a hotel, they paint it orange,
And put some shiny polish on the door hinge.

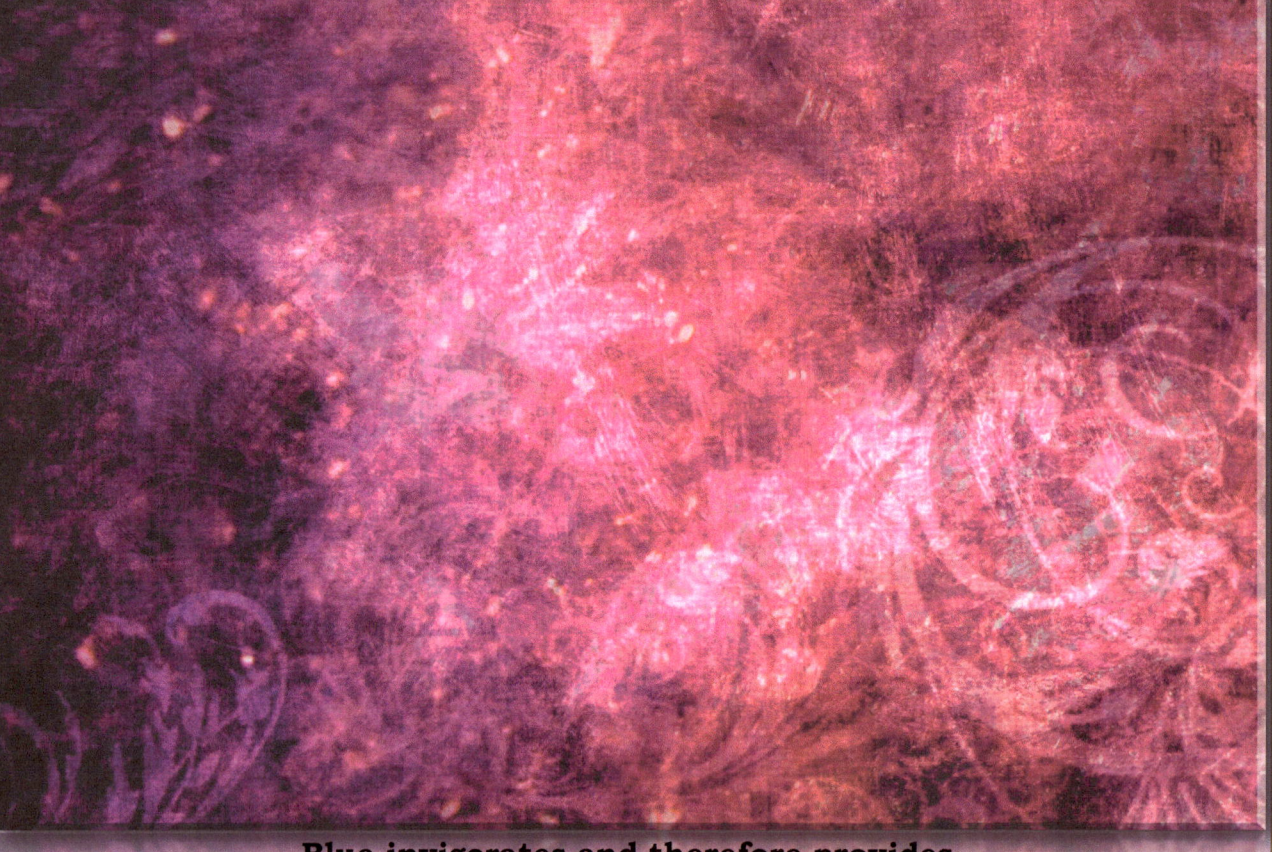

Blue invigorates and therefore provides
Extra strength and power; so blue's on our side
When the home team's locker room is painted
In its hue (visitor's was pink—they fainted).

Blue as was said is good, except on food,
For few foods are blue; so in diet mood,
Put a blue light in your kitchen—and lose
Weight avoiding repulsive looking food.

Pink (red tinted with white) debilitates,
Sapping strength and temper, so that is why
It's used in prison cells and locker rooms,
For it calms the most violent inmates.

What of purple? Well, it's mournful, but too
It's stately, regal, and virginal, new.

Of green, though it's seldom worn, none complain;
And use it in their carpets to stay sane.

The stars are not just white, they scintillate:
Sirius is blue, its companion green;
Betelgeuse, red; many, like Sol, yellow;
Arcturus, orange—all jewels constellate.

Well, as colors go, so then do we, see:
Hues are just differing wavelengths of light
That the brain interprets, in its own right,
For some natural colored necessity.

*May I chance upon a land of strange rainbows*
*Of elfin-hued flowers: red delphiniums,*
*Black tulips, orange fuchsias, white marigolds,*
*Bronze grass, and the legendary blue rose.*

(The Netherworld)

(A Colorful Garden)

The End